WOW!
What Just Happened to Me?

Understanding Your
New Relationship with God

5G REFORMATION
MINISTRIES

PO Box 268

Midlothian, TX 76065, USA

ContactUs@5GMinistries.com

www.5GMinistries.com

HAMILTON HILL
PUBLISHING

Publisher: Hamilton-Hill Publishing

Dallas, TX, USA

ISBN: 978-0-9600407-5-9

Table of Contents

Lesson 1: Born Again 5

Lesson 2: Death & Resurrection 13

Lesson 3: Your New Nature 19

Lesson 4: Spirit, Soul, & Body 27

Lesson 5: Water Baptism 35

Lesson 6: The Baptism of the Holy Spirit 41

Lesson 7: Growing in Christ 49

Answer Key 54

One-Year Bible Reading Plan 62

Introduction

WOW! What Just Happened to Me? is for brand-new believers and seasoned believers who need a solid foundation in the experience of Salvation and an encounter with the Holy Spirit. This study guide is designed to be worked individually, one-on-one, or in a small group setting.

What does it mean to be born again? The Bible teaches that you were united to Christ's death and resurrection when you were born again. Before a resurrection, there must be a death experience. Before you experienced Christ's resurrected life, you had to experience his crucifixion. How was Christ's death applied to you? What happened to your spirit and soul at salvation? What does water baptism signify? Is it essential for salvation? Do you have to be baptized to go to heaven? What is the baptism in the Holy Spirit all about? Can I be baptized in the Holy Spirit and not know it? Is it essential for Salvation? What are the key steps to a vibrant ongoing relationship with Jesus? All these questions and many more will be answered as you work through this discipleship study guide.

At the beginning of each lesson, you will notice a QR code. Please scan the code to watch a 10-minute video overview of the topic. The video does not replace the lesson but gives a summary of what you are about to study.

In the Bible Study section, the Scripture reference is given but not the actual verses. So, grab your Bible or your electronic version and start exploring God's Word.

The Answer Key to each Bible Study is located at the back of the book.

Lesson Born Again 1

WOW! What just happened to me? is a great question. You may have asked that when you prayed and gave your life to the Lord Jesus Christ. Something very significant *did* happen to you. It was not only earth-shattering; it also affected the universe!

The Bible says that when a person gives their life to the God of the universe, the angels in heaven rejoice.[1] So, you have already affected heaven itself!

To understand what happened to you, we must go back many thousands of years to the Garden of Eden. The Bible teaches that God created mankind in His own image,[2] to enjoy a mutual relationship together. In order to have a relationship of love and respect, God gave man the free will to choose. However, man chose to chart his own course and operate independently of God. The Bible calls that sin and rebellion.

"God Himself provided the means of restoring this relationship..."

This independence from a holy God caused spiritual death in mankind. Although every race and tribe of man has attempted to reach out to God, in one form of religion or another, no religion could unite them because of man's sin.

• • • • •

1: **Luke 15:10** – Likewise, I say to you, there is joy in the presence of the angels of God over one sinner who repents.

2: **Genesis 1:26-27** – Then God said, "Let Us make man in Our image, according to Our likeness;" ... So God created man in His own image; in the image of God, He created him; male and female He created them.

God Himself provided the means of restoring this relationship by sending His only Son, the Lord Jesus Christ, to live as a man, to live without sin, and to live in a relationship with His heavenly Father. Jesus willingly was crucified on a cross to receive the judgment of God for mankind's sin. Now, by accepting what Jesus has done for you on the cross, your sins are forgiven, and you are restored back into a relationship with your Creator. This is what has happened to you!

On the third day after His crucifixion, God raised Jesus from the dead because He had no sin of His own. He has now ascended into heaven and will return one day to receive those who have put their trust in Him; those who have received Him as Lord of their lives. That includes you!

The Bible says that if you believe in your heart that Jesus is Lord and are willing to confess this with your mouth, you are saved, made whole, and brought back into a relationship with God.[3]

When you did this, God placed His Holy Spirit in you, and you became spiritually alive. In that sense, you were born again. Your old spiritually dead nature passed away and you received a brand-new nature. You became a brand-new person on the inside. You are now made, once again, into the image of God, something that was lost in the Garden of Eden.

Congratulations! You will spend the rest of your life discovering the depths of this transformation that has happened on the inside of you. This workbook and Bible study guide will help you on that journey.

· · · · ·

3: **Romans 10:9-10** – that if you confess with your mouth the Lord Jesus and believe in your heart that God has raised Him from the dead, you will be saved. For with the heart one believes unto righteousness, and with the mouth, confession is made unto salvation.

Perhaps after reading this lesson, you are not sure if you are born again and have eternal life. If you would like to be sure, here is a simple prayer that you can pray. If you pray this with sincerity, the Bible promises that you will be born again and have a relationship with your heavenly Father.

Jesus, I thank you that you died on the cross for my sins. I confess that you are my Lord and Savior. I believe in my heart that God raised you from the dead. By faith in your Word, I receive you as my Lord right now. Thank you for forgiving my sins and saving me! Thank you for eternal life. Amen.

Based on the promise of God's Word, you are born again and have eternal life.[4]

4: **1 John 5:11-13** – And this is the testimony: that God has given us eternal life, and this life is in His Son. He who has the Son has life; he who does not have the Son of God does not have life. These things I have written to you who believe in the name of the Son of God, that you may know that you have eternal life, and that you may continue to believe in the name of the Son of God.

Lesson 1: Bible Study

1. Read: John 3:3-8

a. According to Jesus, what must happen in order to see the Kingdom of Heaven? (v. 3) _____

_____

b. In verse 5, it states that you must be born physically (of water) and _____ to enter the Kingdom of God.

2. Read: Ephesians 2:1-9

a. What was your spiritual condition before you accepted Jesus as your Lord and Savior? (vs. 1, 5) _____

_____

b. What has happened to you now? (vs. 1, 5)

_____

c. Whose control and power were you under before you surrendered to Christ? (v. 2) _____

_____

d. What were some of the labels that defined you before becoming a Christian? (vs. 2-3) _____

_____

e. What characteristics did God demonstrate towards you that caused you to be born again? (v. 4) _____

_____

f. Can your good works assist you in being born again? (vs. 8-9)

_____

3. Read: Romans 10:8-11

a. What two things did you have to do in order to activate salvation in your life? (vs. 9-10) _____

_____

_____

b. Were you disappointed when you put your trust in Christ? (v. 11)

_____

4. Read: 1 Corinthians 6:9-11

a. The Bible says that the unrighteous will not inherit the Kingdom of God. List some of the activities of the unrighteous. (vs. 9-10)

_____

_____

b. Because you trusted in Jesus Christ, you have been made righteous. What is your current condition? (v. 11)

_____

_____

5. Read: John 1:12-13

a. Because you have believed and received what Christ has done for you, what have you now become? (v. 12) _____

_____

_____

b. What caused you to be born again? (v. 13) _____

_____

_____

6. Read: Galatians 4:6-7

a. Now that you are a child of God, whose Spirit do you have living on the inside of you? (v. 6) _____

b. You are no longer a slave of the devil. What are you now? (v. 7)

_____

_____

Lesson 1: Personal Reflection & Application

1. The following truths from this lesson were brand-new to me.

_____

_____

_____

_____

2. These are the ways that I will apply these new truths in my life.

_____

_____

_____

_____

3. These Scriptures really stood out to me in this study. (Spend some time this week memorizing an important Scripture and thinking about it.)

_____

_____

_____

_____

4. These are the things that I will be talking to God about this week. Jesus said, "Whatever things you ask when you pray, believe that you receive them, and you will have them." *(Mark 11:24)*

_____

_____

_____

_____

•   •   •   •   •

Other Discipleship Study Guides
By Byron Hamilton

Spirit, Soul, & Body

You are a spirit, you have a soul, and you live in a body. Modern psychology only recognizes the soul and body of mankind. Because of such, self-help programs can identify the cause of man's mental and emotional issues but do not provide a long-term solution. The Bible teaches the three elements of man - the spirit, soul, and body. Change happens in the spirit of man where Christ's nature can bring about lasting influence on a person's soul through the renewing of the mind. Every believer needs to know the effects on his spirit and soul when he is united together into Christ's death, burial, and resurrection.

Renewing the Mind

Every believer knows that he/she must be transformed by the renewing of the mind, but how does one renew the mind? The Bible outlines a simple, effortless way to ingest the Word of God on a regular basis in conjunction with the ministry of the Holy Spirit and see the guaranteed results that affect the prosperity of your relationships, finances, mental health, physical health, and overall victory in life. John prayed for believers that they would prosper in all things and be in health even as their souls prospered (3 John 1:2). Learn about the various ways to study the Bible, the purpose of the various Bible versions, and which one is right for you.

Understanding Effective Prayer

It's just as important to know how not to pray as it is to know how to pray effectively. There is a huge difference between praying in an Old Covenant manner and praying as a New Covenant believer. If you don't know the difference, then many of your prayers are ineffective. As a born-again believer, united together with Christ's death, burial, resurrection, and ascension, you can pray with boldness, victory, and faith, based upon your position in Christ. Many of us inadvertently pray from an Old Covenant position, asking God for things that He has already provided for us in the New Covenant. Prayer requests for things that have already been granted by God's grace are never answered. The promises of God are obtained by declared faith and thanksgiving.

All discipleship training guides as well as free material can be found at:
www.5GMinistries.com

Lesson 2
Death
& Resurrection

The Bible teaches that God placed you in Christ when you surrendered your life to Him. You were joined to the Lord and became one spirit with Him.[5] Not only is the Spirit of Christ *in you*, but you are also *in Christ*.

The Bible uses the word *baptism* to describe your union with Christ. *Baptism* doesn't necessarily have anything to do with water. It is a Greek word that simply means "to be joined together with" or "to become one with." *Baptism* is also used in other parts of the New Testament to talk about your union with the Holy Spirit and your union with brothers and sisters in Christ. When you are joined together with something you become identified with it.

When you were joined together with Christ you became identified with His death, burial, resurrection, ascension, His righteousness, power, and His glory. Before there can be a resurrection, there must be a death. And so, a death occurred in you before you experienced Christ's resurrected life. [6]

The Bible says that Christ's death was applied to your old nature. This former nature was disconnected from the life of God, there-

> "The Bible says that Christ's death was applied to your old nature."

• • • • •

5: **1 Corinthians 6:17** – But he who is joined to the Lord is one spirit with Him.

6: **Romans 6:3** – Do you not know that as many of us as were baptized into Christ Jesus were baptized into His death?

fore spiritually dead. This nature is what caused you to be enslaved to sin and unable to break from sin's power and addictions.

The Bible calls this old nature the *old man.*[7] When your old man was put to death, sin's hold was broken off you and you are no longer in bondage to sin.[8] This happened once and for all time. This is incredible news!

After receiving Christ's crucifixion, you received Christ's resurrected life. In place of your old sinful nature, you received the nature of Christ. Christ's life is now your new life! I know this is difficult to believe, but this is what the Bible teaches and it is what happened to you![9]

The apostle Paul said it this way, "My old nature has been crucified with Christ; it is no longer I who live, but it is the life of Christ who now lives in me" (*Galatians* 2:20, paraphrased).

The Bible tells believers that because their old nature is now dead, they don't have to allow sin to have dominion over them.[10] Instead of yielding their bodies to sin, they can now yield to righteousness.[11]

●　●　●　●　●

7: **Romans 6:6** – ...knowing this, that our old man was crucified with Him, that the body of sin might be done away with, that we should no longer be slaves of sin.

8: **Romans 6:7** – For he who has died has been freed from sin.

9: **Colossians 3:3-4** – For you died, and your life is hidden with Christ in God. When Christ who is our life appears, then you also will appear with Him in glory.

10: **Romans 6:12, 14a** – Therefore do not let sin reign in your mortal body, that you should obey it in its lusts. ... For sin shall not have dominion over you.

11: **Romans 6:13** – And do not present your members as instruments of unrighteousness to sin but present yourselves to God as being alive from the dead, and your members as instruments of righteousness to God.

Lesson 2: Bible Study

1. Read: Romans 6:3-6

a. The Greek meaning of *baptism* is "to be immersed in," "to become with," "join together," and "to be overwhelmed with." Use any of these definitions to substitute for the word *baptism* in the following passage. "Or do you not know that as many of us as were _____ Christ Jesus were _____ into His death?" (v. 3)

b. What three things did you identify with when you were united with Christ? (vs. 3-4)

i. _____

ii. _____

iii. _____

c. What died on the inside of you when you were placed into Christ? (v. 6) _____

d. What happened when your old nature was crucified? (v. 6)

_____

_____

2. Read: Romans 6:9-10

Because you were placed into Christ, how does His death and resurrection apply to you? (vs. 8-10) _____

_____

_____

3. Read: Romans 6:11-13

a. Because Christ's death was applied to your old nature what is your relationship now to sin? (vs. 11-12)

_____

_____

b. Your body, mind, and emotions are no longer enslaved to sin, what can you yield yourself to now? (v. 13)

_____

_____

4. Read: Romans 7:2-4

a. The Bible uses the concept of marriage to illustrate your former relationship and your new relationship. What had to happen so you would be free to "marry" another? (v. 2)

_____

_____

b. Who are you "married" to now? (v. 4) _____

5. Read: Colossians 3:1-5

a. Because you died with Christ and were raised with Christ, what do you give your attention to now? (vs. 1-2)

_____

_____

b. Who is your life? (vs. 3-4) _____

c. Now that your old nature is dead, what can also be put to death? (v.5) _____

_____

6. Read: Colossians 3:9-10

a. Why can you stop lying? (v. 9) _____

_____

b. What do you now have in place of the old man? (v. 10)

_____

7. Read: Galatians 2:20

Write out Paul's testimony: _____

_____

_____

_____

_____

_____

_____

_____

_____

_____

_____

Lesson 2: Personal Reflection & Application

1. The following truths from this lesson were brand-new to me.

_____

_____

_____

2. These are the ways that I will apply these new truths in my life.

_____

_____

_____

3. These Scriptures really stood out to me in this study.
(Spend some time this week memorizing an important Scripture and thinking about it.)

_____

_____

_____

4. These are the things that I will be talking to God about this week. Jesus said, "Whatever things you ask when you pray, believe that you receive them, and you will have them." _(Mark 11:24)_

_____

_____

_____

Lesson 3
Your New Nature

The Bible states that when you gave your life to Christ, OLD things passed away and ALL things became new.[12] That's obviously not talking about your body, your memories, your talents, relationships, emotions, and other things that were still with you after you became a Christian. It is speaking about your spirit. In the previous chapter, we learned that you were placed into Christ and His death was applied to your old sinful nature. After that occurred, you then experienced Christ's resurrection and received His life. Your dead spirit was replaced with the life of Christ. All this happened in a moment of time. This is the "all things became new" that this Scripture is talking about.

You were spiritually dead because of sin, disconnected from the life of God.[13] When you yielded yourself to Christ, He gave you His Spirit and His life. Jesus told His disciples that the Holy Spirit who was with them would be in them.[14]

Christ's life is eternal. It doesn't have a beginning nor an end. Thus, by being placed in Christ, you now have eternal life. Your eternal life started the day that you made Jesus Lord of your

> "You were spiritually dead because of sin, disconnected from the life of God."

• • • • •

12: **2 Corinthians 5:17** – Therefore, if anyone is in Christ, he is a new creation; old things have passed away; behold, all things have become new.

13: **Ephesians 2:1** – And you He made alive, who were dead in trespasses and sins.

14: **John 14:16-18** – And I will pray the Father, and He will give you another Helper, that He may abide with you forever — the Spirit of truth, whom the world cannot receive because it neither sees Him nor knows Him; but you know Him, for He dwells with you and will be in you. I will not leave you orphans; I will come to you.

life. It doesn't begin when you physically die. The Bible says that eternal life is in the Son of God. If you have the Son, you have this life. Anyone who does not have the Son of God does not have eternal life.[15]

Because the Holy Spirit is righteous and holy and He now lives in you, your new spiritual, eternal nature is also righteous and holy, without sin.[16] The Bible says that your new nature was created in the very image of God. It is just like the One who created it.[17] And then God sealed your new nature with His Holy Spirit so you would not become contaminated by sin and your own shortcomings.[18]

God no longer looks at you as a sinner. You have been adopted into His heavenly family. He now sees you as His own son or daughter.[19] He no longer sees you as unrighteous; He sees you as possessing His own righteousness.[20]

●　●　●　●　●

15:　**1 John 5:11-12** – And this is the testimony: that God has given us eternal life, and this life is in His Son. He who has the Son has life; he who does not have the Son of God does not have life.

16:　**Ephesians 4:24** – … and that you put on the new man which was created according to God, in true righteousness and holiness.

17:　**Colossians 3:10** – … and have put on the new man who is renewed in knowledge according to the image of Him who created him.

18:　**Ephesians 1:13** – In Him you also trusted, after you heard the word of truth, the gospel of your salvation; in whom also, having believed, you were sealed with the Holy Spirit of promise.

19:　**Galatians 4:6-7** – And because you are sons, God has sent forth the Spirit of His Son into your hearts, crying out, "Daddy, Father!" Therefore you are no longer a slave but a son, and if a son, then an heir of God through Christ.

20:　**2 Corinthians 5:21** – For He made Him who knew no sin to be sin for us, that we might become the righteousness of God in Him.

Lesson 3: Bible Study

1. Read: 2 Corinthians 5:17

a. We use the phrase "passed away" when we refer to someone who has died and is no longer with us. What passed away when you were placed in Christ? _____

_____

b. What did you become when you were placed in Christ?

_____

2. Read: Ephesians 4:24 and Colossians 3:10

How would describe your new self after you were born again?

_____

_____

3. Read: 1 John 5:11-13

a. What else did you receive when you were placed into Christ? (v. 12) _____

b. Do you know that you have eternal life now? _____

_____

c. What must you do to continue to experience eternal life? (v. 13)

_____

4. Read: 1 Corinthians 6:17

What happened when you were joined to the Lord?

5. Read: 2 Corinthians 5:21

a. Where was all your sin placed? _____

_____

b. What did you receive in exchange for your sin?

_____

6. Read: Colossians 3:5, 8, 12-14

a. Now that your old nature is dead and sin no longer has control of you, what are you able to stop doing? (vs. 5 & 8)

_____

_____

b. Now that you have a new nature created in the likeness of God, what are you able to start doing? (vs. 12-14)

_____

_____

7. Read: 1 Corinthians 6:11

a. *Washed* means to be cleansed and made clean.

b. *Sanctified* means to be set apart for God's purpose.

c. *Justified* means to be pardoned, forgiven, and declared free.

Use these meanings to re-write the Scripture referenced above.

_____

_____

_____

Lesson 3: Personal Reflection & Application

1. The following truths from this lesson were brand-new to me.

_____

_____

_____

2. These are the ways that I will apply these new truths in my life.

_____

_____

_____

3. These Scriptures really stood out to me in this study.
(Spend some time this week memorizing an important Scripture and thinking about it.)

_____

_____

_____

4. These are the things that I will be talking to God about this week. Jesus said, "Whatever things you ask when you pray, believe that you receive them, and you will have them." *(Mark 11:24)*

_____

_____

_____

_____

Other Discipleship Study Guides

By Byron Hamilton

The Good Fight of Faith

You will be surprised to learn that the Bible does not teach we are to have faith the size of a mustard seed. Contrary to this popular teaching, Jesus taught that we are to have faith as a mustard seed, which is quite the opposite. Learn about the characteristics of the mustard seed and why Jesus used it to illustrate faith. Faith must be built in a place that is not seen if we are to have the results of faith demonstrated in our tangible world. There are things we must add to our faith to see it grow and there are things we must remove from our lives in order for faith to have its perfect and complete work in us and in our sphere of life. We can all develop the faith that moves mountains and performs miracles.

Kingdom Finances

Jesus uses finances as the least way to determine our faithfulness in the Kingdom of God. In His parable of the unjust servant, the master praised the steward because he used finances to create a better future for himself. Because of this, Jesus remarked that the people of this world are wiser than believers. We must learn how to use worldly finances to prepare for our heavenly reward. The attitude of financial giving changed drastically when the New Covenant replaced the Old Covenant. Now, believers give and receive financially from a position of grace. Financial grace requires an understanding of our position in Christ and the exchange from poverty to prosperity that was accomplished at the cross.

The Believer and the Flesh

"The believer and the flesh" is probably the most misunderstood doctrine in the New Testament. Is the Old Man truly dead? Does the sinful nature have to be put to death daily? Has the new nature of Christ moved in with my former old nature? Is there a perpetual internal warfare going on between my two natures? Do I have to feed one nature and starve the other? Has the flesh been crucified but still lives? If the Old Man is crucified with Christ, why do I feel defeated by sin? In Romans 7, what did Paul mean by not being able to do the things he wanted to do, and doing things he didn't want to do? Let's dive into a full study of the Word of God in the confusing area of the believer and the flesh.

All discipleship training guides as well as free material can be found at:
www.5GMinistries.com

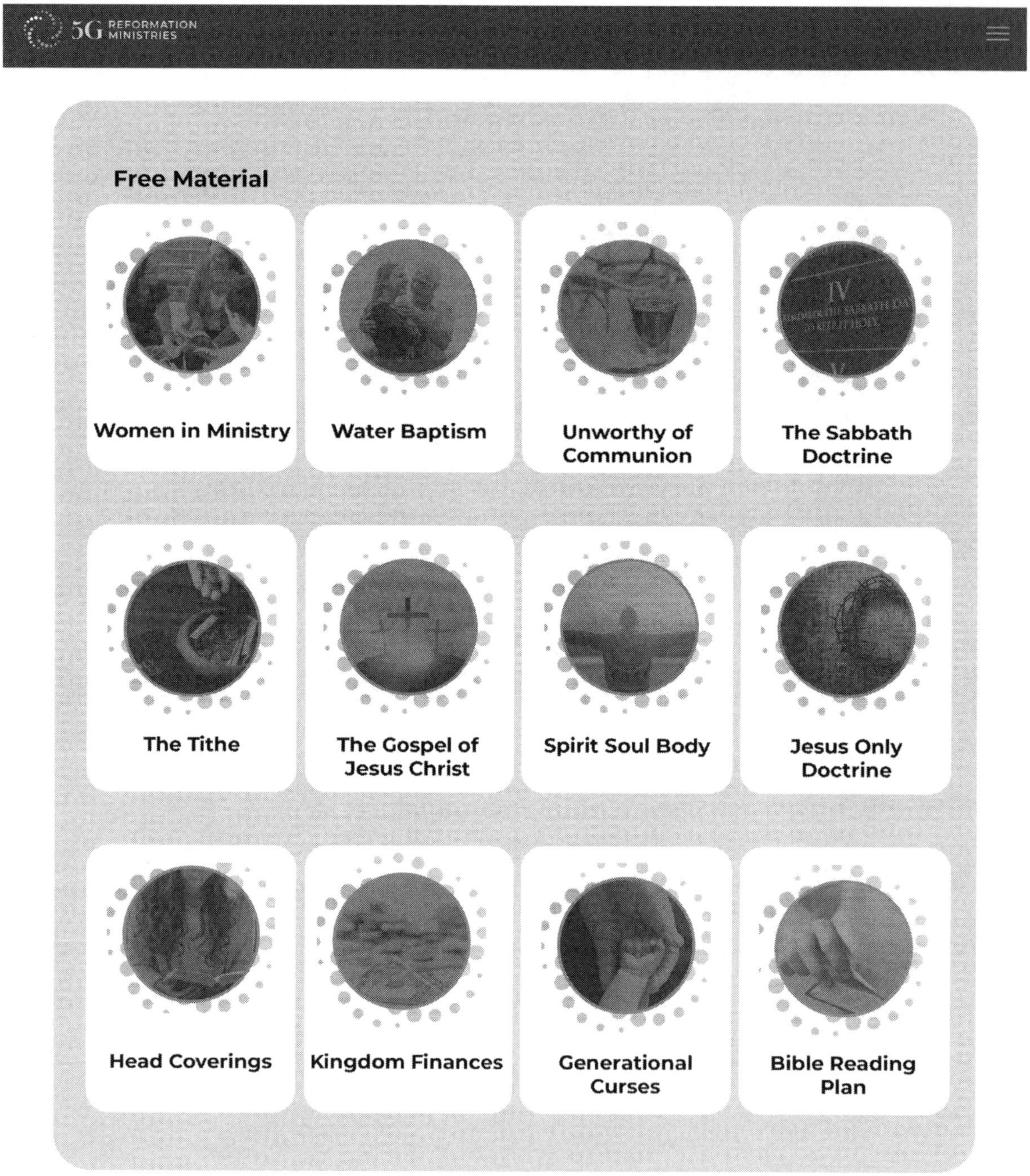

5G REFORMATION MINISTRIES

Free Material

Women in Ministry

Water Baptism

Unworthy of Communion

The Sabbath Doctrine

The Tithe

The Gospel of Jesus Christ

Spirit Soul Body

Jesus Only Doctrine

Head Coverings

Kingdom Finances

Generational Curses

Bible Reading Plan

www.5GMinistries/Ministry-Resources#FreeMaterial

Lesson 4
Spirit, Soul, & Body

God is a triune Being. That means He exists as one God but in three distinct persons. Mankind was created in His image.[21] We also have been created as three distinct parts, but one person. We are a spirit, we have a soul, and we live in a body. The apostle Paul mentions these components when he prayed for believers, that their total spirit, soul, and body would be preserved blameless.[22] What happened to these parts of you when you were born again?

Let's start with the spirit. The Bible says that you were spiritually dead because of sin. So, although you had a spirit, it was cut off from the life of God, thus spiritually dead. It is like an unplugged lamp. The lamp exists but there is no electrical current to it - no juice - it's lifeless. This was your nature, held in bondage to sin, and ruled by the devil. This is the part of you that was born again when you gave your life to Christ. The Bible says that because of God's love and mercy, He brought new life to you.[23] As we discussed earlier, in your spirit, all things

> "God is a triune Being. That means He exists as one God but in three distinct persons."

· · · · ·

21: **Genesis 1:27** – So God created man in His own image; in the image of God, He created him; male and female He created them.

22: **1 Thessalonians 5:23** – Now may the God of peace Himself sanctify you completely; and may your whole spirit, soul, and body be preserved blameless at the coming of our Lord Jesus Christ.

23: **Ephesians 2:4-5** – But God, who is rich in mercy, because of His great love with which He loved us, even when we were dead in trespasses, made us alive together with Christ (by grace you have been saved).

were made new. You now have a brand-new spirit, a brand-new nature. You now have the nature of Christ. In your spirit you are identical to Jesus Christ.[24] In your spirit, you were made righteous and holy. You will not get any more holy in your spirit than the day you were born again. This is how your heavenly Father sees you. You relate to Him in the spirit and by the spirit.[25]

Now let's talk about your soul. This is your personality, made up of your mind, will, and emotions. It is through the soul that you express who you are. This part of you was not born again when you received Jesus Christ. You still deal with many of the same thought processes, emotions, and decisions. But now your soul comes under the influence of your new spirit, the new you. Your spiritually dead self was put to death through Christ's crucifixion. The Bible calls that part of you the *old man* or the *carnal nature*. Because your soul used to function under the control of your old nature, it still has many patterns of thinking, feelings, and decisions left over from your former self. So now, God is in the process of renewing your soul to the image of who you are in your spirit man. As you renew your mind to the Word of God your soul is transformed more and more into the image of Jesus Christ.

Your body is the physical tent in which you live while here on this earth. It is the last part of you that will be changed. When you finish this life, you will shed this temporal tent and your spirit and soul will go into the presence of God. The Bible says that the body is dead without the spirit.[26] The Holy Spirit in you is the guarantee from God that you will get a resurrected body just like Jesus when He returns.

●　●　●　●　●

24:　**1 John 4:17c** – ... because as He is, so are we in this world.

25:　**John 4:24** – God is Spirit, and those who worship Him must worship in spirit and truth.

26:　**James 2:26** – For as the body without the spirit is dead, so faith without works is dead also.

Lesson 4: Bible Study

1. Read: 1 Thessalonians 5:23

You are a three-part being as mentioned by Paul in this passage. What are those components?

a. _____

b. _____

c. _____

2. Read: Genesis 2:16-17, 5:5

a. What part of Adam and Eve died when they rebelled against God? _____

b. How old was Adam when he died physically? _____

3. Read: Ephesians 2:1, 5

a. What state were you in before you came to Christ?

_____

b. What happened when you were joined with Christ?

_____

4. Read: Ephesians 2:2-3

a. When you were spiritually dead, who did your old nature serve? (v. 2) _____

_____

b. What two things were you called?

(v. 2) _____

(v. 3) _____

c. When you were spiritually dead, what did your old nature do?

(v. 3) _____

5. Read: Ephesians 1:13-14, Romans 8:23

a. What happened to you after you believed in the Gospel of Jesus Christ? (v. 13) _____

_____

b. We still have an inheritance. What remains to be redeemed? (v. 14, Rom 8:23) _____

6. Read: James 1:21-22

a. What things are the believers told to stop doing? (v. 21)

_____

b. What are you told to receive? (v. 21) _____

_____

c. With what attitude? (v. 21) _____

d. What is that able to do? (v. 21) _____

_____

e. Save means to "make whole." Your soul will be made whole, or complete, by doing what? (v. 22) _____

_____

7. Read: 1 Peter 1:9, 22-23

a. We have complete salvation in our spirit, but what are we waiting on? (v. 9) _____

_____

b. What happens to our soul as we obey the truth of God's Word and love one another? (v. 22) _____

c. How were you born again in your spirit? (v. 23)

_____

_____

8. Read: 2 Peter 1:13-14

a. What did Peter call his body? _____

b. What was he going to do with it soon? _____

_____

• • • • •

Lesson 4: Personal Reflection & Application

1. The following truths from this lesson were brand-new to me.

_____

_____

_____

2. These are the ways that I will apply these new truths in my life.

_____

_____

_____

3. These Scriptures really stood out to me in this study.
(Spend some time this week memorizing an important Scripture
and thinking about it.)

_____

_____

_____

4. These are the things that I will be talking to God about this week.
Jesus said, "Whatever things you ask when you pray, believe that
you receive them, and you will have them." *(Mark 11:24)*

_____

_____

_____

_____

Other Discipleship Study Guides
By Byron Hamilton

Proverbs to Live By

There are 30 subjects in the book of Proverbs. The
conventional reading of this most loved book of the Bible has
the reader jumping from one proverb to another and one
topic to another. This creative, novel, thematic approach to
Proverbs enables the reader to stay focused on one theme for

each chapter, drilling deep into the rich treasures of wisdom, knowledge, understanding, and discernment. Learn about the seven pillars of wisdom and how to place them in sequential order as you enact wise decisions and build success and prosperity.

Jesus' Final Teachings

Five of the most popular chapters in the book of John (chapters 13 through 17) outline in detail the final teachings of Jesus to His closest disciples on the night that He was betrayed and arrested. This seven-subject study focuses on specific revelations never revealed by Jesus before in His ministry but left for His last night on the planet. You will join the disciples in the dimly lit upper room and feast intently on the final words of the Master.

Merging the Gospels

Although there are four Gospel writers, most material is covered by only one, two, or three of the writers. Very few events in the Gospel books are covered by all four authors. In fact, up until the final week of Jesus, only the miracle of feeding the 5,000 is recorded by all four Gospel writers! That is an amazing discovery. Even when several Gospel writers record the same event, the story is told from different perspectives revealing different details. It is only as we combine the writings of all four witnesses into one manuscript that we fully understand the teachings, parables, and ministry of the Lord Jesus Christ. For the first time, read the Gospels as one document and receive the corresponding revelation for the first time!

All discipleship training guides as well as free material can be found at:
www.5GMinistries.com

Lesson 5
Water Baptism

When you say the word *baptism* you are actually saying a Greek word. When the Bible was translated into English in the 1600s, the Greek word *baptizō* was just modified to look like an English word. Therefore, we do not have a good definition for the word. However, from its use in Greek literature and the Bible we can deduce that it means to *submerge, to wash or bathe, to become one with or inseparably identified with.*

We see a pattern in the Bible that people were baptized in water very soon after they were born again or after they received the fullness of the Holy Spirit. After the evangelist Philip shared the Gospel with the Ethiopian Minister of Finance, the minister responded, "Here is water. What's stopping me from being baptized now?"[27] On another occasion, the apostle Peter shared the Gospel with the first non-Jewish family. After the Holy Spirit came upon them, Peter responded to his Jewish team members, "Is anyone going to deny them water to be baptized?"[28]

"We see a pattern in the Bible that people were baptized in water..."

In Philip's conversation with the Ethiopian official, we learn the qualifications of baptism. To his question about being baptized, Philip responded, "If you believe with all your heart, you may." To which the Ethiopian replied, "I believe that Jesus Christ is the

● ● ● ● ●

27: **Acts 8:36** – Now as they went down the road, they came to some water. And the eunuch said, "See, here is water. What hinders me from being baptized?"

28: **Acts 10:47** – Then Peter answered, "Can anyone forbid water, that these should not be baptized who have received the Holy Spirit just as we have?"

Son of God!" *(Acts 8:37).* So, believing in the Lord Jesus Christ and what He did for you on the cross qualifies you for being baptized. That answers the questions: *Can babies be baptized?* And, *How old do you have to be to be baptized?* "If you believe with all your heart, you may."

So, baptism is for those who are believers. That also answers another question: *If you're not baptized, will you go to heaven?* Another person who is recorded in the New Testament as being baptized is the Philippian jailor. He asked the apostle Paul, "What must I do to be saved?" To which Paul replied, "Believe on the Lord Jesus Christ and you will be saved!" *(Acts 16:30-31).* Believing on the Lord Jesus Christ is what gets you saved, born again, and eternal life.

Water baptism is an outward demonstration and public witness of what has already taken place on the inside of you. As we have already learned, when you were joined to the Lord at salvation, His death and resurrection were applied to your life. His crucifixion was applied to your old man, (your old sinful nature), and it died. His resurrection was applied to you as well. You now have a brand-new nature, that is, the nature of Christ. So, you identify with both the death and resurrection of Jesus Christ.

This is what you are demonstrating when you go down into the water, get completely covered, and then come up again. It's a picture of death, burial, and resurrection. It's identifying with Jesus Christ. It's illustrating what has already taken place on the inside of you, in your spirit. And that's why we submerge in water rather than sprinkling with water. It is also a public way of letting all your friends, family, and relatives know where you stand spiritually.

So, you can see why baptism is so closely tied to your salvation experience. If you haven't been baptized yet, what are you waiting for? "If you believe with all your heart, you may."

Lesson 5: Bible Study

1. Read: Matthew 28:18-20

What were the three final commands given by Jesus to the disciples? (vs. 19-20)

a. _____

b. _____

c. _____

2. Read: Acts 16:30-33

a. What was the question that the Philippian jailer asked? (v. 30)

_____

_____

_____

b. What was Paul's answer? (v. 31) _____

_____

c. What happened to the jailer and his family after they all became believers? (v. 33) _____

_____

3. Read: Acts 8:35-38

a. What was the question that the Ethiopian asked after he believed? (v. 36) _____

_____

b. What was Philip's answer? (v. 37) _____

_____

c. Did Philip immerse the man in water or sprinkle him? (v. 38)

_____

4. Read: Romans 6:3-6

We have learned that one of the definitions of the Greek word *baptizō* is to "become one with."

a. Rewrite verse 3. Substitute this meaning for the word baptism.

"Or do you not know that as many of us as _____

_____

Jesus Christ _____ His death."

b. If you became united with or joined together with his death, you have also been joined together with His _____ (v. 5)

c. How is the truth of death, burial, and resurrection with Christ illustrated by water baptism? _____

_____

_____

5. Read: 1 Peter 3:21

One group of believers (Noah's family) was delivered through the Great Flood. This was a picture of being delivered through the water of baptism.

a. What is water baptism not? _____

_____

b. Obeying the ordinance of baptism is the response of a

_____ towards God.

6. Read: Acts 2:38

How closely is baptism associated with salvation?

_____

_____

• Have you ever been baptized? _____

• Perhaps you were baptized as a baby or small child. Would you like to be re-baptized now that you know its meaning and significance? _____

Lesson 5: Personal Reflection & Application

1. The following truths from this lesson were brand-new to me.

_____

_____

_____

2. These are the ways that I will apply these new truths in my life.

_____

_____

_____

3. These Scriptures really stood out to me in this study.
(Spend some time this week memorizing an important Scripture and thinking about it.)

_____

_____

_____

4. These are the things that I will be talking to God about this week. Jesus said, "Whatever things you ask when you pray, believe that you receive them, and you will have them." _(Mark 11:24)_

_____

_____

_____

_____

Lesson 6
The Baptism of the Holy Spirit

In our previous lesson, we learned about water baptism. But we also learned that baptism means more than just a ceremony with water. The Greek word means to *be immersed with* or *to become united together with*.

Along with water baptism, the Bible also speaks about being baptized in the Holy Spirit. This means to be fully immersed, filled, enveloped, united with, and empowered by the Holy Spirit.

On His last night with the disciples, Jesus had promised them that the Holy Spirit, who had been with them, would be *in* them.[29] Then, after His resurrection, Jesus appeared to them and breathed out the Holy Spirit, telling them to, "Receive the Holy Spirit."[30] This is when they were spiritually born again.

> "Along with water baptism, the Bible also speaks about being baptized in the Holy Spirit."

Earlier, Jesus had told Nicodemus, a Jewish religious leader, that a person has to be born physically *and* born again by the Holy Spirit in order to enter the Kingdom of God. So, it's impossible for anyone to be saved (born again) without an encounter with the Holy Spirit. Until we are born again, we are spiritually dead. We

• • • • •

29: **John 14:16-17c** – And I will pray the Father, and He will give you another Helper, that He may abide with you forever — ... for He dwells with you and will be in you.

30: **John 20:22** – And when He had said this, He breathed on them, and said to them, "Receive the Holy Spirit."

have to receive the Holy Spirit's life to be made spiritually alive. This is salvation.

However, although the disciples were born again, Jesus told them not to start any ministry until they were empowered by the Holy Spirit.[31] So, they gathered together in an upper room in Jerusalem for ten days after Jesus' ascension. On the Day of Pentecost, the Holy Spirit came upon 120 believers, and they began to speak in other tongues (languages) and glorify God.[32] This is what the Bible calls the baptism in the Holy Spirit. It is subsequent to salvation and is God's empowering presence for ministry.

When the early church scattered because of persecution, Philip, one of the early church workers, left Jerusalem and went to Samaria to preach the Gospel. Many people were born again and were baptized in water. But they had not received the baptism of the Holy Spirit. Upon hearing about this revival in Samaria, Peter and John went there, laid their hands on the believers, and they received the fullness of the Holy Spirit.

On another occasion, the apostle Paul met some disciples in Ephesus and asked them if they had received the Holy Spirit since they had believed. They hadn't. So, Paul laid His hands on them, they were baptized in the Holy Spirit and began to speak in tongues and prophesy.[33]

Spiritual gifts are activated through the baptism of the Holy Spirit. Believers are empowered for ministry through the bap-

* * * * *

31: **Acts 1:8** – But you shall receive power when the Holy Spirit has come upon you; and you shall be witnesses to Me in Jerusalem, and in all Judea and Samaria, and to the end of the earth.

32: **Acts 2:4** – And they were all filled with the Holy Spirit and began to speak with other tongues, as the Spirit gave them utterance.

33: **Acts 19:6** – And when Paul had laid hands on them, the Holy Spirit came upon them, and they spoke with tongues and prophesied.

tism of the Holy Spirit. It is God's empowering presence.

As His child, your loving heavenly Father wants to give you the supernatural power you need to live victoriously in the Kingdom of God. All you have to do is ask, believe, and receive! You must believe to receive. Someone has said, "Believe and receive, doubt and do without." The Bible says, "Therefore I say to you, whatever things you ask when you pray, believe that you receive them, and you will have them" *(Mark 11:24)*.

If you would like to receive the baptism of the Holy Spirit, pray this prayer:

> *Heavenly Father, I recognize my need for Your power to live this new life. I ask You to baptize me and fill me with Your Holy Spirit. By faith, I receive Him right now! I worship You and honor You. Holy Spirit, I welcome You in my life.*

Congratulations! Now you're filled with God's supernatural power.

Some syllables from a language you don't recognize will/may rise from your heart to your mouth. This is the gift of speaking in tongues. The Bible says we can pray in the spirit, and we can pray with understanding (1 Cor. 14:15). The Holy Spirit is giving you the utterance or the syllables, but you must speak them forth. Acts 2:4 records that the disciples spoke what the Holy Spirit was giving them. As you speak them out loud by faith, you're releasing God's power from within and building yourself up in the Spirit. You can do this whenever and wherever you like.

Lesson 6: Bible Study

1. Read: John 20:21-22

a. When did the disciples first receive the Holy Spirit? (v. 22)

_____

_____

b. What is the similarity between Jesus' ministry and the disciples' ministry? (v. 21) _____

_____

2. Read: Acts 1:4-8

a. Why did Jesus command His disciples to wait in Jerusalem? (v.4) _____

_____

b. What was the "Promise of the Father"? (v. 5) _____

_____

c. What would the disciples receive after they were baptized with the Holy Spirit? (v. 8) _____

3. Read: Acts 2:1-4

a. On the Day of Pentecost, what were the disciples filled with? (v. 4) _____

b. What was one of the signs that they had received the baptism of the Holy Spirit? (v. 4) _____

_____

4. Read: Acts 19:1-7

a. What had the disciples in Ephesus not received after they had believed? (v. 2) _____

_____

b. What did Paul do first with these disciples? (v. 5)

_____

_____

c. What did Paul do after these believers were baptized in water? (v. 6) _____

_____

d. What was the evidence that they had been baptized in the Holy Spirit? (v. 6) _____

_____

5. Read: 1 Corinthians 14:1-5

a. What are you doing when you are speaking in tongues? (v. 2)

_____

_____

b. What is the purpose of prophesying? (v. 3) _____

_____

c. When you speak privately in tongues, who is being built up and edified? (v. 4) _____

d. If someone has the spiritual gift of speaking in tongues publicly to the church, what also must happen? (v. 5) _____

6. Read: Jude 1:20

How do you build up yourself and edify yourself? _____

_____

7. Read: 1 Corinthians 14:14-15

a. When you pray in tongues, do you understand it with your natural mind? (v. 14) _____

b. What is Paul's conclusion about praying and singing in the Holy Spirit? (v. 15) _____

_____

_____

Lesson 6: Personal Reflection & Application

1. The following truths from this lesson were brand-new to me.

_____

_____

_____

2. These are the ways that I will apply these new truths in my life.

_____

_____

_____

3. These Scriptures really stood out to me in this study.
(Spend some time this week memorizing an important Scripture and thinking about it.)

_____

_____

_____

4. These are the things that I will be talking to God about this week. Jesus said, "Whatever things you ask when you pray, believe that you receive them, and you will have them." _(Mark 11:24)_

_____

_____

_____

Join us online for live teaching, group interaction, and ministry. Students say, "You'll never be the same after completing any of the courses!" Commit one night per week for a 6- or 8-week course and dive deep into the Word of God.

This is what you've been praying for!
www.5GMinistries/Kingdom-University

Lesson 7
Growing in Christ

Let's review what has happened to you.

1. Because of God's mercy and love, you have been delivered from the power of darkness and placed into the Kingdom of God.

2. Your past, present, and future sins have been paid for through the death of Jesus Christ on the cross. You have been forgiven and pardoned from all your sins and failures.

3. God has placed His Holy Spirit on the inside of you. You are now a child of God. You're a brand-new person, in right standing with God. In your spirit, you have been recreated into the image of Jesus Christ.

4. Because of Christ's resurrection, you now have eternal life. Although you will die physically, you'll never die spiritually because you have eternal life now.

5. When Jesus rose from the dead, He defeated the power and authority of the devil over you. You now are equipped with the authority and power of the Lord Jesus Christ who lives in you by His Holy Spirit.

6. Nothing can separate you from the love of God. If He sent His own Son to die for you when you were separated from Him, how much more can you experience His love now that you are His child?

7. Your spirit is perfect. Your soul is being transformed into the image of Christ. One day, when Christ returns, you will be taken into heaven to enjoy His presence forever. You will receive a new resurrected body.

Your journey has just started! The starting gun has gone off and you have begun the race. However, this race is not a sprint, it's a marathon.

The Holy Spirit is in you to guide you, counsel you, and lead you into all truth. You will hear His quiet peaceful voice within. The Bible says that God's overriding plan for you is to conform you into the image of His Son, Jesus Christ. So, although God has direction for you in where you should live, what church to go to, your relationships, schooling, jobs, careers, finances, and so on, His ultimate plan is to make you like Jesus.[34] You have been chosen for this purpose. And God is so awesome that He is able to take every situation, even the bad ones, and bring good out of them so that you can be transformed in your thinking, your emotions, and decision-making. You will become more and more like Jesus Christ.[35]

Although you have been delivered from Satan's power and Jesus has defeated the devil, he is still around. His only power over you is through lies and deception.[36] It will be important that you begin to regularly read the Bible, particularly the New Testament. It is also important that you find a good church where they teach the Bible and help to disciple you. By regularly reading God's Word, spending time with God's people, and talking with the Holy Spirit in prayer, you will begin to grow strong in your relationship with God. You will be able to stand against the devil's temptation to return to the lifestyle that once held you in bondage.

You will want to tell your friends, family members, and others about your new relationship with God and what has actually hap-

* * * * *

34: **Romans 8:29** – For whom He foreknew, He also predestined to be conformed to the image of His Son, that He might be the firstborn among many brethren.

35: **Romans 8:28** – And we know that all things work together for good to those who love God, to those who are the called according to His purpose.

36: **Ephesians 6:11** – Put on the whole armor of God, that you may be able to stand against the wiles (deceitful trickery) of the devil.

pened to you. They will all see the difference in you because you have a new nature. Some of them will want to know how they can have a relationship with God as well. But others will think you've gone nuts and won't want anything to do with you. You may even lose some friends. But be assured, God will give you new ones. Jesus Himself calls you His friend and He said, "For whoever does the will of God is My family."[37]

In Matthew 13, Jesus told a parable about a farmer who sowed seeds in different types of soils. The first type of soil was a footpath that was so hard it could not take the seed. Jesus said the seed represented the Word of God. This illustrates those who do not receive the Word of God because they do not understand it. You are not this type of soil. You have received the Word of God into your life.

The second type of soil was rocky. The seed penetrated this stony soil, but the roots could not go down very far. When the sun brought its heat, the small plant withered because it did not have a good root system. This type of soil illustrates people who initially receive the Word of God but because of persecution and hardship, they give up.

The third type of soil was full of weeds. The weeds competed with the small plant for nutrients. Although the roots went down further in *this* soil, the roots of the weeds and thorns choked out the plant and it could not mature. Jesus said that this type of soil represents the things that compete for the Word of God in your life; things like the deceitfulness of getting rich, the pursuit of pleasures, distractions, and the basic cares of life. These all took priority over the Word of God in this soil and the plant did not fulfill its purpose.

* * * * *

37: **Mark 3:35** – For whoever does the will of God is My brother and My sister and mother.

However, some seed fell onto good soil, and it was able to produce a good, successful harvest. I pray that you will guard your heart against the distractions of life and the pressure from other people so that you mature spiritually and enjoy a prosperous and successful life in your relationship with God.

Jesus said to prioritize the Kingdom of God in your life and then all the things that you are pursuing will come into your life anyway.[38] The key to success and prosperity is giving God, His Word, His Spirit, and His people preeminence in your life. This is how you truly make Jesus lord of your life. He is your Savior, but He needs to be Lord as well.

The Gospel of John is a great place to start reading God's Word. Read through John's Gospel several times before you begin reading elsewhere in the New Testament. A one-year Bible reading plan is provided for you at the end of this study guide. It will enable you to read through the New Testament four times in a year.

Remember, your Christian life is not a sprint, it's a marathon. The Bible says that Jesus is the starting point of your race and the One who will ensure that you finish your race.[39] Many have gone on before you and have completed their races, even some of your family members. They are pulling for you, cheering you on! So, toss aside anything that will slow you down, anything that will trip you up, make the commitment, and run with determination. And never give up! You are a winner, not a loser.

●   ●   ●   ●   ●

38: **Matthew 6:32b-33** – ... Your heavenly Father knows that you need all these things. But seek first the kingdom of God and His righteousness, and all these things shall be added to you.

39: **Hebrews 12:1-2a** – Therefore we also, since we are surrounded by so great a cloud of witnesses, let us lay aside every weight, and the sin which so easily ensnares us, and let us run with endurance the race that is set before us, looking unto Jesus, the author and finisher of our faith.

Join us online to interact with Leesa's prophetic blogs. Ask Byron a biblical question, get a response, and join the discussion!

www.5GMinistries/Blog

Answer Key

Lesson 1: Born Again

Question 1
    a. You must be born again.
    b. Spiritually.

Question 2
    a. I was spiritually dead because of sin.
    b. I have been made spiritually alive.
    c. I was under the control of the prince and the power of the air.
    d. I was a son of disobedience. I was a child of God's wrath.
    e. His mercy and great love.
    f. No, it is by His grace so that no one can boast.

Question 3
    a. Confess with my mouth the Lord Jesus and believe in my heart that God raised Him from the dead.
    b. No, I was not put to shame.

Question 4
    a. Fornicators (sexually immoral), idolaters, adulterers, homosexuals and sodomites (same gender sex), thieves, covetous (greedy graspers), drunkards (hard drinking), revilers (abusive language, foulmouthed), extortioners (greed & robbery).
    b. Washed clean, set apart for God (sanctified), pardoned by God (justified).

Question 5
    a. I am now a child of God.
    b. I was born again by the will of God.

Question 6
   a. I have the Spirit of God's Son.
   b. I am a son of God and an heir of God.

Lesson 2: Death & Resurrection

Question 1
   a. Or do you not know that as many of us as were joined together with Christ Jesus became one with His death? (or other similar definitions).
   b. i. Death.
      ii. Burial.
      iii. Resurrection.
   c. My old man.
   d. The body of sin was done away with, and I am no longer a slave to sin.

Question 2
   Because I was placed in Christ, His death was applied to me, and my old sinful nature died with Him. I also participated in His resurrection. I now have His life and I live for God (or similar).

Question 3
   a. I am also dead to sin, so I do not need to have sin reign over me.
   b. I can yield myself to God. I don't have to yield to unrighteousness but to righteousness.

Question 4
   a. Death had to occur.
   b. Christ.

Question 5
  a. I think about things that are above, not on the things of
     this earth.
  b. Christ is my life.
  c. The activities that were associated with my old sinful
     nature: sexual immorality, impurity, lust, evil desires,
     and greed.

Question 6
  a. Because I have put off the old nature with his deeds.
  b. The new man.

Question 7
  I have been crucified with Christ; it is no longer I who live,
  but Christ lives in me; and the life which I now live in the
  flesh I live by faith in the Son of God, who loved me and gave
  Himself for me.

Lesson 3: Your New Nature

Question 1
  a. Old things have passed away (the old man).
  b. A new creation.

Question 2
  My new self is created like God in true righteousness and
  holiness. It is being renewed in knowledge in the image
  of God.

Question 3
  a. Eternal life.
  b. Yes.
  c. I must continue to believe in the name of the Lord
     Jesus Christ.

Question 4

I became one spirit with Him.

Question 5

a. My sin was placed on Jesus. He became sin.
b. The righteousness of God.

Question 6

a. I can stop fornication, sexual immorality, impurity, evil desires, covetousness, greed, anger, wrath, rage, malice, blasphemy, filthy language, lies (or similar).
b. I can put on tender mercies, compassion, kindness, humility, meekness, gentleness, longsuffering, patience, bear with one another, forgive one another, and love (or similar).

Question 7

And such were some of you. But you were cleansed, but you were set apart for God's purposes, and you were pardoned, forgiven, and declared free, all in the name of the Lord Jesus and by the Spirit of our God (or similar).

Lesson 4: Spirit, Soul, & Body

Question 1

a. Spirit.
b. Soul.
c. Body.

Question 2

a. They spiritually died.
b. 930.

Question 3

a. Spiritually dead.

b. I became spiritually alive.

Question 4

a. "The prince and power of the air."
b. A son of disobedience and a child of wrath.
c. Lived by the lust of the flesh, fulfilling the desires of the flesh and the mind.

Question 5

a. I was sealed with the Holy Spirit of promise.
b. Our bodies.

Question 6

a. Living in moral filth and wickedness.
b. Receive the implanted Word of God.
c. With meekness/humility.
d. Save my soul.
e. Being a doer of the Word and not just a hearer.

Question 7

a. The salvation of our souls.
b. We purify our souls.
c. I was born again with incorruptible seed through the Word of God.

Question 8

a. A tent.
b. He was going to put off his tent.

Lesson 5: Water Baptism

Question 1
    a. Go and make disciples of all nations.
    b. Baptize them in the name of the Father, Son, & Holy Spirit.
    c. Teach them to observe the things that Jesus taught.

Question 2
    a. What must I do to be saved?
    b. Believe in the Lord Jesus Christ and you will be saved.
    c. They were all baptized in water.

Question 3
    a. What hinders me from being baptized?
    b. If you believe with all your heart, you may.
    c. He was immersed in water.

Question 4
    a. Or do you not know that as many of us became one with Christ Jesus became one with His death?
    b. Resurrection.
    c. In water baptism, you go down into the water that illustrates the death and burial. Then you come up out of the water that illustrates resurrection.

Question 5
    a. It is not the removal of filth from the body.
    b. Good conscience.

Question 6
It is very much associated with salvation. It demonstrated the remission and forgiveness of sin and the preparation for the Holy Spirit.

Lesson 6: The Baptism of the Holy Spirit

Question 1
   a. After Christ's resurrection and before His ascension.
   b. As God sent Christ out into the world, so Christ sends us out into the world.

Question 2
   a. They were to wait for the Promise of the Father.
   b. The baptism of the Holy Spirit.
   c. Power.

Question 3
   a. The Holy Spirit.
   b. Speaking in other tongues.

Question 4
   a. The Holy Spirit.
   b. We baptized them in the name of the Lord Jesus.
   c. He laid his hands on them and they received the Holy Spirit.
   d. They spoke in tongues and prophesied.

Question 5
   a. You are not speaking to men; you are speaking to God.
   b. To give edification, strengthening, encouragement, and comfort to men.
   c. You edify yourself.
   d. There must be an interpretation in a public setting.

Question 6
By praying in the Holy Spirit.

Question 7

a. No.

b. I can pray in the Spirit, and I can pray with my understanding. I can sing in the Spirit, and I can sing with my understanding.

Bible Reading Plan

This plan will enable you to read through the New Testament four times in a year by reading two chapters per day.

✓	Day	Reading
Matthew		
❏	1	1 & 2
❏	2	3 & 4
❏	3	5 & 6
❏	4	7 & 8
❏	5	9 & 10
❏	6	11 & 12
❏	7	13 & 14
❏	8	15 & 16
❏	9	17 & 18
❏	10	19 & 20
❏	11	21 & 22
❏	12	23 & 24
❏	13	25 & 26
❏	14	27 & 28
Acts		
❏	15	1 & 2
❏	16	3 & 4
❏	17	5 & 6
❏	18	7 & 8
❏	19	9 & 10
❏	20	11 & 12
❏	21	13 & 14
❏	22	15 & 16
❏	23	17 & 18
❏	24	19 & 20
❏	25	21 & 22
❏	26	23 & 24
❏	27	25 & 26
❏	28	27 & 28
Romans		
❏	29	1 & 2
❏	30	3 & 4
❏	31	5 & 6
❏	32	7 & 8
❏	33	9 & 10
❏	34	11 & 12
❏	35	13 & 14
❏	36	15 & 16

✓	Day	Reading
1 Corinthians		
❏	37	1 & 2
❏	38	3 & 4
❏	39	5 & 6
❏	40	7 & 8
❏	41	9 & 10
❏	42	11 & 12
❏	43	13 & 14
❏	44	15 & 16
2 Corinthians		
❏	45	1 & 2
❏	46	3 & 4
❏	47	5 & 6
❏	48	7 & 8
❏	49	9 & 10
❏	50	11 - 13
Galatians		
❏	51	1 & 2
❏	52	3 & 4
❏	53	5 & 6
Ephesians		
❏	54	1 & 2
❏	55	3 & 4
❏	56	5 & 6
Philippians		
❏	57	1 & 2
❏	58	3 & 4
Colossians		
❏	59	1 & 2
❏	60	3 & 4
1 Thessalonians		
❏	61	1 & 2
❏	62	3 - 5
2 Thessalonians		
❏	63	1 - 3
1 Timothy		
❏	64	1 & 2
❏	65	3 & 4
❏	66	5 & 6

✓	Day	Reading
2 Timothy		
❏	67	1 & 2
❏	68	3 & 4
Titus		
❏	69	1 & 2
❏	70	3 & Philemon
Hebrews		
❏	71	1 & 2
❏	72	3 & 4
❏	73	5 & 6
❏	74	7 & 8
❏	75	9 & 10
❏	76	11 - 13
James		
❏	77	1 & 2
❏	78	3 - 5
1 Peter		
❏	79	1 & 2
❏	80	3 - 5
2 Peter		
❏	81	1 - 3
1 John		
❏	82	1 & 2
❏	83	3 - 5
❏	84	2, 3 John, Jude
Revelation		
❏	85	1 & 2
❏	86	3 & 4
❏	87	5 & 6
❏	88	7 & 8
❏	89	9 & 10
❏	90	11 & 12
❏	91	13 & 14
❏	92	15 & 16
❏	93	17 & 18
❏	94	19 & 20
❏	95	21 & 22

✓	Day	Reading
Mark		
❏	96	1 & 2
❏	97	3 & 4
❏	98	5 & 6
❏	99	7 & 8
❏	100	9 & 10
❏	101	11 & 12
❏	102	13 & 14
❏	103	15 & 16
Acts		
❏	104	1 & 2
❏	105	3 & 4
❏	106	5 & 6
❏	107	7 & 8
❏	108	9 & 10
❏	109	11 & 12
❏	110	13 & 14
❏	111	15 & 16
❏	112	17 & 18
❏	113	19 & 20
❏	114	21 & 22
❏	115	23 & 24
❏	116	25 & 26
❏	117	27 & 28
Romans		
❏	118	1 & 2
❏	119	3 & 4
❏	120	5 & 6
❏	121	7 & 8
❏	122	9 & 10
❏	123	11 & 12
❏	124	13 & 14
❏	125	15 & 16
1 Corinthians		
❏	126	1 & 2
❏	127	3 & 4
❏	128	5 & 6
❏	129	7 & 8
❏	130	9 & 10
❏	131	11 & 12
❏	132	13 & 14
❏	133	15 & 16

✓	Day	Reading
2 Corinthians		
☐	134	1 & 2
☐	135	3 & 4
☐	136	5 & 6
☐	137	7 & 8
☐	138	9 & 10
☐	139	11 - 13
Galatians		
☐	140	1 & 2
☐	141	3 & 4
☐	142	5 & 6
Ephesians		
☐	143	1 & 2
☐	144	3 & 4
☐	145	5 & 6
Philippians		
☐	146	1 & 2
☐	147	3 & 4
Colossians		
☐	148	1 & 2
☐	149	3 & 4
1 Thessalonians		
☐	150	1 & 2
☐	151	3 - 5
2 Thessalonians		
☐	152	1 - 3
1 Timothy		
☐	153	1 & 2
☐	154	3 & 4
☐	155	5 & 6
2 Timothy		
☐	156	1 & 2
☐	157	3 & 4
Titus		
☐	158	1 & 2
☐	159	3 & Philemon
Hebrews		
☐	160	1 & 2
☐	161	3 & 4
☐	162	5 & 6
☐	163	7 & 8
☐	164	9 & 10
☐	165	11 - 13
James		
☐	166	1 & 2
☐	167	3 - 5

✓	Day	Reading
1 Peter		
☐	168	1 & 2
☐	169	3 - 5
2 Peter		
☐	170	1 - 3
1 John		
☐	171	1 & 2
☐	172	3 - 5
☐	173	2, 3 John, Jude
Revelation		
☐	174	1 & 2
☐	175	3 & 4
☐	176	5 & 6
☐	177	7 & 8
☐	178	9 & 10
☐	179	11 & 12
☐	180	13 & 14
☐	181	15 & 16
☐	182	17 & 18
☐	183	19 & 20
☐	184	21 & 22
Luke		
☐	185	1 & 2
☐	186	3 & 4
☐	187	5 & 6
☐	188	7 & 8
☐	189	9 & 10
☐	190	11 & 12
☐	191	13 & 14
☐	192	15 & 16
☐	193	17 & 18
☐	194	19 & 20
☐	195	21 & 22
☐	196	23 & 24
Acts		
☐	197	1 & 2
☐	198	3 & 4
☐	199	5 & 6
☐	200	7 & 8
☐	201	9 & 10
☐	202	11 & 12
☐	203	13 & 14
☐	204	15 & 16
☐	205	17 & 18
☐	206	19 & 20
☐	207	21 & 22
☐	208	23 & 24
☐	209	25 & 26
☐	210	27 & 28

✓	Day	Reading
Romans		
☐	211	1 & 2
☐	212	3 & 4
☐	213	5 & 6
☐	214	7 & 8
☐	215	9 & 10
☐	216	11 & 12
☐	217	13 & 14
☐	218	15 & 16
1 Corinthians		
☐	219	1 & 2
☐	220	3 & 4
☐	221	5 & 6
☐	222	7 & 8
☐	223	9 & 10
☐	224	11 & 12
☐	225	13 & 14
☐	226	15 & 16
2 Corinthians		
☐	227	1 & 2
☐	228	3 & 4
☐	229	5 & 6
☐	230	7 & 8
☐	231	9 & 10
☐	232	11 - 13
Galatians		
☐	233	1 & 2
☐	234	3 & 4
☐	235	5 & 6
Ephesians		
☐	236	1 & 2
☐	237	3 & 4
☐	238	5 & 6
Philippians		
☐	239	1 & 2
☐	240	3 & 4
Colossians		
☐	241	1 & 2
☐	242	3 & 4
1 Thessalonians		
☐	243	1 & 2
☐	244	3 - 5
2 Thessalonians		
☐	245	1 - 3
1 Timothy		
☐	246	1 & 2
☐	247	3 & 4
☐	248	5 & 6

✓	Day	Reading
2 Timothy		
☐	249	1 & 2
☐	250	3 & 4
Titus		
☐	251	1 & 2
☐	252	3 & Philemon
Hebrews		
☐	253	1 & 2
☐	254	3 & 4
☐	255	5 & 6
☐	256	7 & 8
☐	257	9 & 10
☐	258	11 - 13
James		
☐	259	1 & 2
☐	260	3 - 5
1 Peter		
☐	261	1 & 2
☐	262	3 - 5
2 Peter		
☐	263	1 - 3
1 John		
☐	264	1 & 2
☐	265	3 - 5
☐	266	2, 3 John, Jude
Revelation		
☐	267	1 & 2
☐	268	3 & 4
☐	269	5 & 6
☐	270	7 & 8
☐	271	9 & 10
☐	272	11 & 12
☐	273	13 & 14
☐	274	15 & 16
☐	275	17 & 18
☐	276	19 & 20
☐	277	21 & 22
John		
☐	278	1, 2 & 3
☐	279	4, 5 & 6
☐	280	7, 8 & 9
☐	281	10, 11 & 12
☐	282	13, 14 & 15
☐	283	16, 17 & 18
☐	284	19, 20 & 21

✓	Day	Reading
		Acts
☐	285	1 & 2
☐	286	3 & 4
☐	287	5 & 6
☐	288	7 & 8
☐	289	9 & 10
☐	290	11 & 12
☐	291	13 & 14
☐	292	15 & 16
☐	293	17 & 18
☐	294	19 & 20
☐	295	21 & 22
☐	296	23 & 24
☐	297	25 & 26
☐	298	27 & 28
		Romans
☐	299	1 & 2
☐	300	3 & 4
☐	301	5 & 6
☐	302	7 & 8
☐	303	9 & 10
☐	304	11 & 12
☐	305	13 & 14
☐	306	15 & 16
		1 Corinthians
☐	307	1 & 2
☐	308	3 & 4
☐	309	5 & 6
☐	310	7 & 8
☐	311	9 & 10
☐	312	11 & 12
☐	313	13 & 14
☐	314	15 & 16

✓	Day	Reading
		2 Corinthians
☐	315	1 & 2
☐	316	3 & 4
☐	317	5 & 6
☐	318	7 & 8
☐	319	9 & 10
☐	320	11 - 13
		Galatians
☐	321	1 & 2
☐	322	3 & 4
☐	323	5 & 6
		Ephesians
☐	324	1 & 2
☐	325	3 & 4
☐	326	5 & 6
		Philippians
☐	327	1 & 2
☐	328	3 & 4
		Colossians
☐	329	1 & 2
☐	330	3 & 4
		1 Thessalonians
☐	331	1 & 2
☐	332	3 - 5
		2 Thessalonians
☐	333	1 - 3

✓	Day	Reading
		1 Timothy
☐	334	1 & 2
☐	335	3 & 4
☐	336	5 & 6
		2 Timothy
☐	337	1 & 2
☐	338	3 & 4
		Titus
☐	339	1 & 2
☐	340	3 & Philemon
		Hebrews
☐	341	1 & 2
☐	342	3 & 4
☐	343	5 & 6
☐	344	7 & 8
☐	345	9 & 10
☐	346	11 - 13
		James
☐	347	1 & 2
☐	348	3 - 5
		1 Peter
☐	349	1 & 2
☐	350	3 - 5
		2 Peter
☐	351	1 - 3

✓	Day	Reading
		1 John
☐	352	1 & 2
☐	353	3 - 5
☐	354	2, 3 John, Jude
		Revelation
☐	355	1 & 2
☐	356	3 & 4
☐	357	5 & 6
☐	358	7 & 8
☐	359	9 & 10
☐	360	11 & 12
☐	361	13 & 14
☐	362	15 & 16
☐	363	17 & 18
☐	364	19 & 20
☐	365	21 & 22

5GMinistries.com

Made in the USA
Columbia, SC
15 April 2024

34309742R00037